Contents

What to Do

Choose a face

Remember the colour you have chosen.

When you see your face on the page, you are the LEADER.

The LEADER reads the text in the speech bubbles.

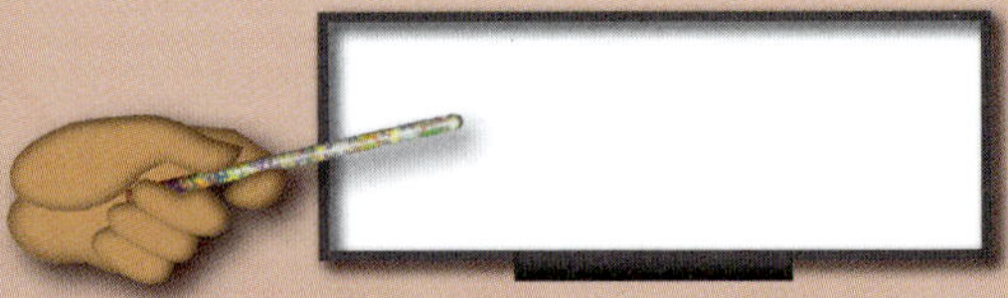

There are extra words and questions to help you on the teacher's whiteboard. The LEADER reads these aloud.

When you see this stop sign, the LEADER reads it aloud.

You might need:

- to look at the WORD HELP on pages 20–22;
- to look at the LOCATION HELP on page 23;
- an atlas.

If you are the **LEADER**, follow these steps:

1 PREDICT

Think about what is on the page.

- Say to your group:

"I am looking at this page and I think it is going to be about…"

- Tell your group:

"Read the page to yourselves."

2 CLARIFY

Talk about words and their meaning.

- Say to your group:

"Are there any words you don't know?"

"Is there anything else on the page you didn't understand?"

- Talk about the words and their meanings with your group.
- Read the whiteboard.

- Ask your group to find the LET'S CHECK word in the WORD HELP on pages 20–22. Ask them to read the meaning of the word aloud.

3 ASK QUESTIONS

Talk about how to find out more.

- Say to your group:

"Who has a question about what we have read?"

- Question starters are: how..., why..., when..., where..., what..., who...
- Read the question on the whiteboard and talk about it with your group.

4 SUMMARISE

Think about who and what the story was mainly about.

When you get to pages 16–17, you can talk to a partner or write and draw on your own.

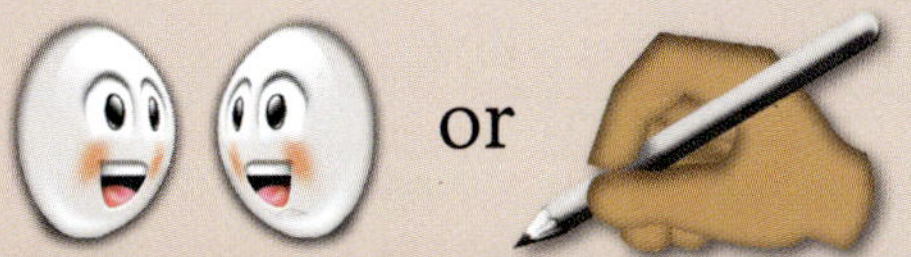

Traffic Jams – A Problem

I am looking at this page and I think it is going to be about… because…

Traffic jams can happen anywhere. People can get very **frustrated** if they are stuck in a traffic jam.

If a person was driving a skycar, they wouldn't have to worry about traffic jams. Drivers could just move over to the side of the road, get their car ready and zoom into the sky. The traffic jam would be far beneath them.

Are there any words you don't know?

Let's check: frustrated

Who has a question about what we have read?

What do you think drivers would have to do to get the skycar ready to fly?

7 出口
建国门桥
2.1km
5 出口
朝阳门桥
a **model** of the skycar in the city
This page was
mainly about
fact
fact
STOP
My predictions were right/wrong because . . .

Inventing A Flying Car

I am looking at this page and I think it is going to be about... because...

For many years, people have been trying to invent a car that flies. Some were too dangerous. Some were too expensive, and others just did not work.

But one day, an **inventor** named Gilo Cardozo put a motor onto a sand **buggy**. The motor had a big **propeller** and a sail. As Gilo zoomed over the ground, the buggy went up into the air. Gilo had turned the sand buggy into a flying car.

an early flying car **invention**

Are there any words you don't know?

Let's check: buggy

Who has a question about what we have read?

Why do you think some flying cars were too dangerous?

Gilo Cardozo puts a propeller onto the motor of his sand buggy.

The Skycar

I am looking at this page and I think it is going to be about… because...

Gilo's flying car is called the skycar. It has a racing bike engine. The engine moves the skycar along when it is on the ground. The engine uses **fuel** made from plants.

When the car is flying, a **parasail** helps to move it along. As the car speeds over the ground the parasail fills up with air. If the parasail gets damaged or **collapses**, the skycar uses a **parachute**. The parachute will **unfold** so that the skycar can glide safely back down to the ground.

Are there any words you don't know?

Let's check: parasail

Who has a question about what we have read?

Why do you think people might use fuel made from plants?

1. The parasail lies behind the skycar.

2. A propeller pushes air into the parasail.

3. The parasail rises into the air.

4. The skycar speeds up and lifts into the sky.

This page was mainly about fact fact

STOP

My predictions were right/wrong because . . .

Testing the Skycar

I am looking at this page and I think it is going to be about… because…

The skycar had to be tested to make sure it was safe. It was important to see if it could fly long **distances** as well.

So Gilo Cardozo and his team went on a long journey to Timbuktu. This was a dangerous journey. They had to cross the sea and travel over a desert. It was hot and dusty in the desert. They were a long way from anywhere.

Are there any words you don't know?

Let's check: distances

Who has a question about what we have read?

Why do you think it was important to test the car on a long journey?

The skycar crosses the sea between Spain and Africa.

The skycar takes off over the sea.

A Successful Journey

I am looking at this page and I think it is going to be about… because…

The most dangerous part of the journey was crossing the sea. The strong winds made the skycar swing around, but no one was hurt.

Some people thought that the trip would fail. It didn't. The skycar was a success. It could drive on motorways. It could go over sand **dunes** and rocky ground. And, it could fly safely a long way, too.

Are there any words you don't know?

Let's check: dunes

Who has a question about what we have read?

Do you think that the test for the skycar was a good one? Why do you think that?

The skycar is seen here leaving the shores of Spain.

The skycar makes a successful landing after crossing the sea.

This page was mainly about

fact

fact

STOP

My predictions were right/wrong because . . .

A Future for Skycars

I am looking at this page and I think it is going to be about… because…

Skycars aren't used yet to fly in and out of cities. They are noisy and they need space to take off.

Skycars would be useful in many ways. They are easier to fly than a helicopter and not as **expensive**. They could get to places where helicopters and other **vehicles** couldn't.

One day, skycars could be zooming around in the sky like giant birds.

Are there any words you don't know?

Let's check: vehicles

Who has a question about what we have read?

What do you think some of the benefits of a skycar would be?

The skycar is a good model for flying cars in the **future**. These are Gilo Cardozo's new skycar designs.

This page was mainly about fact fact

STOP
My predictions were right/wrong because . . .

Something to Think About 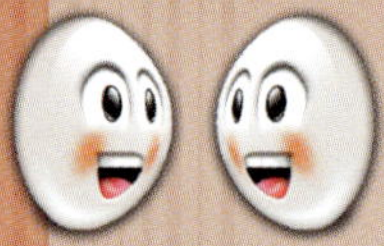 or 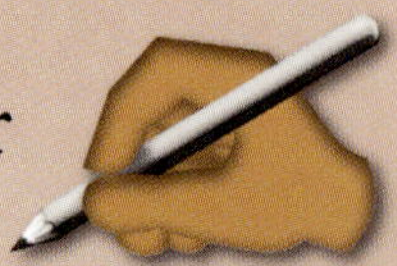

A skycar might be useful because . . .

Think about why a skycar might be useful, and why it might not. Talk about your ideas with a partner, or write them down.

A skycar might not be useful because . . .

Do You Need to Find an Answer?

You could go to . . .

Do You Want to Find Out More?

You could look in books or on the internet. These key words could help you:

- Gilo Cardozo
- parajet
- parasail
- skycar

Word Help

Dictionary

buggy	a small, light vehicle powered by a motor
collapses	falls down or falls in
distances	far away
dunes	a hill of sand made by wind or water
expensive	costing a lot of money
frustrated	feeling upset or annoyed
fuel	something that is burned to give power or heat
future	a time that hasn't come yet
invention	something that has never been made before
inventor	someone who invents something new

model	an example that shows a style or design
parachute	a large piece of cloth that opens up like an umbrella when a cord is pulled
paramotor	a name for the motor which pushes the skycar through the air
parasail	a special type of large parachute that is attached to a boat or car
propeller	a set of blades that spin around
unfold	to open something and spread it out
vehicles	anything that takes people or objects from one place to another

Word Help

Thesaurus

damaged	harmed, broken
giant	enormous, massive
glide	fly, float, drift
journey	trip, voyage
noisy	loud, deafening
speeds	races
stuck	trapped, caught, jammed
zoom	dive, rocket, sail

Location Help

Test Route

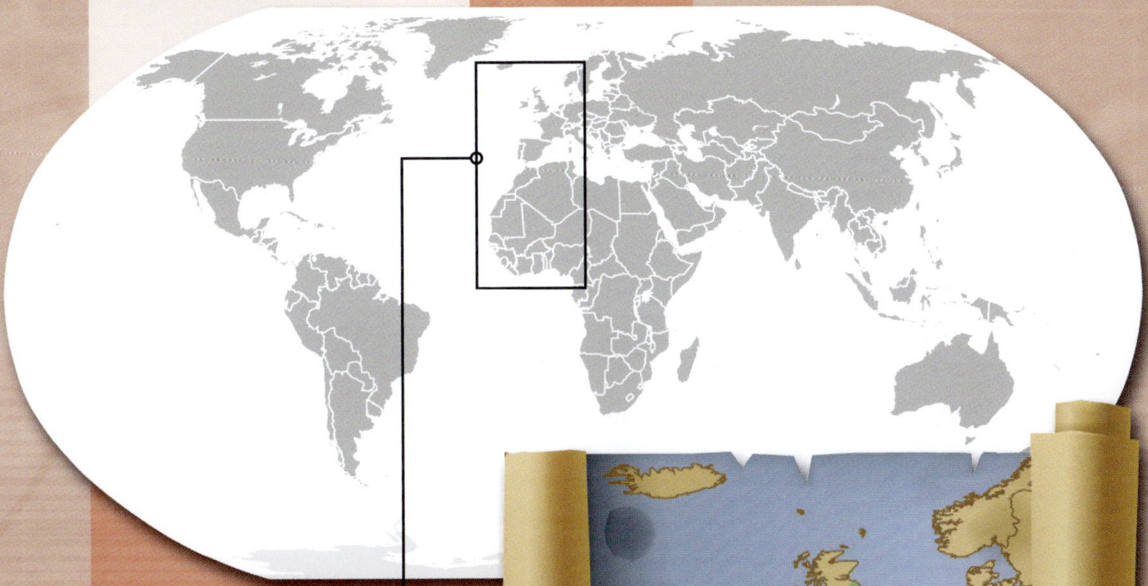

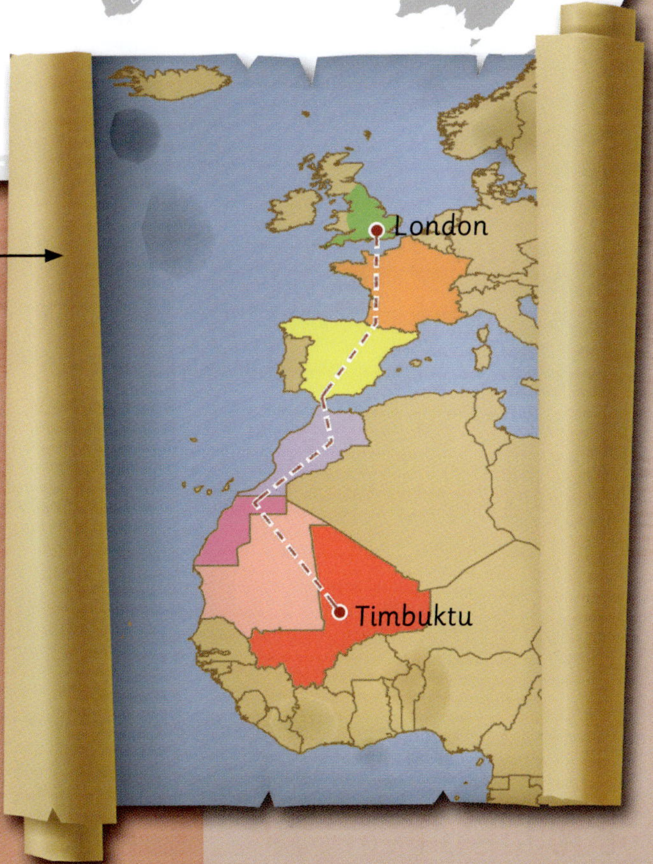

Countries the skycar travelled through:

- England
- France
- Spain
- Morocco
- Western Sahara
- Mauritania
- Mali

Index